The Real Book Multi-Tracks Vol. 5

For C, B♭, E♭ & Bass Clef Instruments

Jazz Funk

Play-Along

To access online content visit:
www.halleonard.com/mylibrary

Enter Code
1787-2635-7147-2050

ISBN 978-1-4950-7477-6

For more information on the Real Book series, including community forums, please visit
www.OfficialRealBook.com

For all works contained herein:
Unauthorized copying, arranging, adapting, recording, Internet posting, public performance,
or other distribution of the music in this publication is an infringement of copyright.
Infringers are liable under the law.

Visit Hal Leonard Online at
www.halleonard.com

Contact us:
Hal Leonard
7777 West Bluemound Road
Milwaukee, WI 53213
Email: info@halleonard.com

In Europe, contact:
Hal Leonard Europe Limited
42 Wigmore Street
Marylebone, London, W1U 2RN
Email: info@halleonardeurope.com

In Australia, contact:
Hal Leonard Australia Pty. Ltd.
4 Lentara Court
Cheltenham, Victoria, 3192 Australia
Email: info@halleonard.com.au

Contents

ALLIGATOR BOGALOO

- LOU DONALDSON

C VERSION

SOLO ON C BLUES
AFTER SOLOS, D.S. AL ⊕
(PLAY PICKUPS) (TAKE REPEAT)

© 1967 (Renewed) EMI UNART CATALOG INC.
All Rights Administered by EMI UNART CATALOG INC. (Publishing) and ALFRED MUSIC (Print)
All Rights Reserved   Used by Permission

THE CHICKEN

- ALFRED ELLIS

© 1969 (Renewed) GOLO PUBLISHING COMPANY
All Rights Administered by UNICHAPPELL MUSIC, INC.
All Rights Reserved   Used by Permission

6

Cissy Strut

— Arthur Neville/Leo Nocentelli/
George Porter/Joseph Modeliste, Jr.

C Version

Copyright © 1969 Screen Gems-EMI Music Inc.
Copyright Renewed
All Rights Administered by Sony/ATV Music Publishing LLC, 424 Church Street, Suite 1200, Nashville, TN 37219
International Copyright Secured   All Rights Reserved

Cold Duck Time

C VERSION

— EDDIE HARRIS

Copyright © 1969 (Renewed) Seventh House Ltd.
All Rights Reserved   Used by Permission

COMIN' HOME BABY

– BOB DOROUGH/BENJAMIN TUCKER

Copyright © 1962 Sincere Music Co. and BENGLO MUSIC INC.
Copyright Renewed
All Rights Controlled and Administered by IRVING MUSIC, INC.
All Rights Reserved   Used by Permission

MERCY, MERCY, MERCY

– JOSEF ZAWINUL

C VERSION

FINE

Copyright © 1966 Zawinul Enterprises LLC
Copyright Renewed
All Rights Administered by Songs Of Kobalt Music Publishing
All Rights Reserved   Used by Permission

PUT IT WHERE YOU WANT IT

— JOE SAMPLE

C VERSION

Copyright © 1971 Chrysalis Music Ltd.
Copyright Renewed
All Rights Administered by BMG Rights Management (US) LLC
All Rights Reserved   Used by Permission

SIDEWINDER

- LEE MORGAN

Copyright © 1959 (Renewed) Conrad Music (BMI)
U.S. Rights owned by Arc/Conrad Music LLC (Administered by BMG Rights Management (US) LLC)
International Copyright Secured   All Rights Reserved

Tom Cat

— TOM SCOTT

C VERSION

FINE

SOLO [A] [B] [C] [D]
AFTER SOLOS, D.S. AL FINE
(PLAY PICKUPS)

Copyright © 1974 HOLLENBECK MUSIC
Copyright Renewed
All Rights Administered by IRVING MUSIC, INC.
All Rights Reserved   Used by Permission

WATERMELON MAN

(MED.)

C VERSION

— HERBIE HANCOCK

AFTER SOLOS, D.S. AL ⊕
(NO REPEAT)

Copyright © 1973 (Renewed) Hancock Music
International Copyright Secured   All Rights Reserved

ALLIGATOR BOGALOO

- LOU DONALDSON

(MED. FAST)

Bb VERSION

SOLO ON D BLUES
AFTER SOLOS, D.S. AL ⊕
(PLAY PICKUPS) (TAKE REPEAT)

© 1967 (Renewed) EMI UNART CATALOG INC.
All Rights Administered by EMI UNART CATALOG INC. (Publishing) and ALFRED MUSIC (Print)
All Rights Reserved   Used by Permission

The Chicken

- Alfred Ellis

© 1969 (Renewed) GOLO PUBLISHING COMPANY
All Rights Administered by UNICHAPPELL MUSIC, INC.
All Rights Reserved Used by Permission

Cissy Strut

— Arthur Neville/Leo Nocentelli/
George Porter/Joseph Modeliste, Jr.

Copyright © 1969 Screen Gems-EMI Music Inc.
Copyright Renewed
All Rights Administered by Sony/ATV Music Publishing LLC, 424 Church Street, Suite 1200, Nashville, TN 37219
International Copyright Secured   All Rights Reserved

Cold Duck Time

Bb VERSION

— EDDIE HARRIS

Copyright © 1969 (Renewed) Seventh House Ltd.
All Rights Reserved   Used by Permission

COMIN' HOME BABY

— BOB DOROUGH/BENJAMIN TUCKER

AFTER SOLOS, D.S. AL ⊕
(PLAY PICKUPS) (TAKE REPEAT)

TAG

Copyright © 1962 SINCERE MUSIC CO. and BENGLO MUSIC INC.
Copyright Renewed
All Rights Controlled and Administered by IRVING MUSIC, INC.
All Rights Reserved   Used by Permission

MERCY, MERCY, MERCY

– JOSEF ZAWINUL

FINE

Copyright © 1966 Zawinul Enterprises LLC
Copyright Renewed
All Rights Administered by Songs Of Kobalt Music Publishing
All Rights Reserved   Used by Permission

PUT IT WHERE YOU WANT IT

- JOE SAMPLE

Copyright © 1971 Chrysalis Music Ltd.
Copyright Renewed
All Rights Administered by BMG Rights Management (US) LLC
All Rights Reserved   Used by Permission

Sidewinder

– Lee Morgan

Copyright © 1959 (Renewed) Conrad Music (BMI)
U.S. Rights owned by Arc/Conrad Music LLC (Administered by BMG Rights Management (US) LLC)
International Copyright Secured   All Rights Reserved

Tom Cat

— TOM SCOTT

Copyright © 1974 HOLLENBECK MUSIC
Copyright Renewed
All Rights Administered by IRVING MUSIC, INC.
All Rights Reserved   Used by Permission

Watermelon Man

(MED.)

Bb Version

— Herbie Hancock

Copyright © 1973 (Renewed) Hancock Music
International Copyright Secured   All Rights Reserved

ALLIGATOR BOGALOO

- LOU DONALDSON

SOLO ON A BLUES
AFTER SOLOS, D.S. AL ⊕
(PLAY PICKUPS) (TAKE REPEAT)

© 1967 (Renewed) EMI UNART CATALOG INC.
All Rights Administered by EMI UNART CATALOG INC. (Publishing) and ALFRED MUSIC (Print)
All Rights Reserved   Used by Permission

The Chicken

— ALFRED ELLIS

© 1969 (Renewed) GOLO PUBLISHING COMPANY
All Rights Administered by UNICHAPPELL MUSIC, INC.
All Rights Reserved   Used by Permission

CISSY STRUT

- Arthur Neville/Leo Nocentelli/
George Porter/Joseph Modeliste, Jr.

Eb Version

(MED. SLOW)

Copyright © 1969 Screen Gems-EMI Music Inc.
Copyright Renewed
All Rights Administered by Sony/ATV Music Publishing LLC, 424 Church Street, Suite 1200, Nashville, TN 37219
International Copyright Secured   All Rights Reserved

Cold Duck Time

Eb Version

— Eddie Harris

Copyright © 1969 (Renewed) Seventh House Ltd.
All Rights Reserved   Used by Permission

Comin' Home Baby

— Bob Dorough/Benjamin Tucker

Copyright © 1962 Sincere Music Co. and Benglo Music Inc.
Copyright Renewed
All Rights Controlled and Administered by IRVING MUSIC, INC.
All Rights Reserved   Used by Permission

MERCY, MERCY, MERCY

— JOSEF ZAWINUL

Eb VERSION

Copyright © 1966 ZAWINUL Enterprises LLC
Copyright Renewed
All Rights Administered by Songs Of Kobalt Music Publishing
All Rights Reserved   Used by Permission

Put It Where You Want It

(Med.)

— Joe Sample

Eb Version

AFTER SOLOS, D.S. AL ⊕
(TAKE REPEAT)

Copyright © 1971 Chrysalis Music Ltd.
Copyright Renewed
All Rights Administered by BMG Rights Management (US) LLC
All Rights Reserved   Used by Permission

SIDEWINDER

– LEE MORGAN

Copyright © 1959 (Renewed) Conrad Music (BMI)
U.S. Rights owned by Arc/Conrad Music LLC (Administered by BMG Rights Management (US) LLC)
International Copyright Secured   All Rights Reserved

Copyright © 1974 HOLLENBECK MUSIC
Copyright Renewed
All Rights Administered by IRVING MUSIC, INC.
All Rights Reserved   Used by Permission

Watermelon Man

Eb Version

- Herbie Hancock

Copyright © 1973 (Renewed) Hancock Music
International Copyright Secured   All Rights Reserved

ALLIGATOR BOGALOO

- LOU DONALDSON

SOLO ON C BLUES
AFTER SOLOS, D.S. AL ⊕
(PLAY PICKUPS) (TAKE REPEAT)

© 1967 (Renewed) EMI UNART CATALOG INC.
All Rights Administered by EMI UNART CATALOG INC. (Publishing) and ALFRED MUSIC (Print)
All Rights Reserved   Used by Permission

THE CHICKEN

— ALFRED ELLIS

C BASS VERSION

© 1969 (Renewed) GOLO PUBLISHING COMPANY
All Rights Administered by UNICHAPPELL MUSIC, INC.
All Rights Reserved   Used by Permission

CISSY STRUT

Copyright © 1969 Screen Gems-EMI Music Inc.
Copyright Renewed
All Rights Administered by Sony/ATV Music Publishing LLC, 424 Church Street, Suite 1200, Nashville, TN 37219
International Copyright Secured   All Rights Reserved

Cold Duck Time

C BASS VERSION

— EDDIE HARRIS

*OPTIONAL 8VA THROUGHOUT

AFTER SOLOS, D.S. AL ⊕
(PLAY PICKUPS) (TAKE REPEAT)

Copyright © 1969 (Renewed) Seventh House Ltd.
All Rights Reserved   Used by Permission

Comin' Home Baby

- Bob Dorough/Benjamin Tucker

C BASS VERSION

Copyright © 1962 SINCERE MUSIC CO. and BENGLO MUSIC INC.
Copyright Renewed
All Rights Controlled and Administered by IRVING MUSIC, INC.
All Rights Reserved   Used by Permission

MERCY, MERCY, MERCY

— JOSEF ZAWINUL

C BASS VERSION

FINE

Copyright © 1966 Zawinul Enterprises LLC
Copyright Renewed
All Rights Administered by Songs Of Kobalt Music Publishing
All Rights Reserved   Used by Permission

PUT IT WHERE YOU WANT IT

- JOE SAMPLE

C BASS VERSION

AFTER SOLOS, D.S. AL ⊕
(TAKE REPEAT)

Copyright © 1971 Chrysalis Music Ltd.
Copyright Renewed
All Rights Administered by BMG Rights Management (US) LLC
All Rights Reserved   Used by Permission

Sidewinder

(FAST)

– Lee Morgan

C BASS VERSION

BASS & RHYTHM – CONT. SIM.

REPEAT HEAD IN/OUT

(MELODY OUT ON REPEATS)

FINE

Copyright © 1959 (Renewed) Conrad Music (BMI)
U.S. Rights owned by Arc/Conrad Music LLC (Administered by BMG Rights Management (US) LLC)
International Copyright Secured   All Rights Reserved

TOM CAT

— TOM SCOTT

C BASS VERSION

Copyright © 1974 HOLLENBECK MUSIC
Copyright Renewed
All Rights Administered by IRVING MUSIC, INC.
All Rights Reserved   Used by Permission

WATERMELON MAN

C BASS VERSION

- HERBIE HANCOCK

AFTER SOLOS, D.S. AL ⊕
(NO REPEAT)

Copyright © 1973 (Renewed) Hancock Music
International Copyright Secured   All Rights Reserved

THE REALBOOK MULTI-TRACKS

TODAY'S BEST WAY TO PRACTICE JAZZ!
Accurate, easy-to-read lead sheets and professional, customizable audio tracks accessed online for 10 songs

1. MAIDEN VOYAGE PLAY-ALONG

Autumn Leaves • Blue Bossa • Doxy • Footprints • Maiden Voyage • Now's the Time • On Green Dolphin Street • Satin Doll • Summertime • Tune Up.
00196616 Book with Online Media..........$17.99

2. MILES DAVIS PLAY-ALONG

Blue in Green • Boplicity (Be Bop Lives) • Four • Freddie Freeloader • Milestones • Nardis • Seven Steps to Heaven • So What • Solar • Walkin'.
00196798 Book with Online Media..........$17.99

3. ALL BLUES PLAY-ALONG

All Blues • Back at the Chicken Shack • Billie's Bounce (Bill's Bounce) • Birk's Works • Blues by Five • C-Jam Blues • Mr. P.C. • One for Daddy-O • Reunion Blues • Turnaround.
00196692 Book with Online Media..........$17.99

4. CHARLIE PARKER PLAY-ALONG

Anthropology • Blues for Alice • Confirmation • Donna Lee • K.C. Blues • Moose the Mooche • My Little Suede Shoes • Ornithology • Scrapple from the Apple • Yardbird Suite.
00196799 Book with Online Media..........$17.99

5. JAZZ FUNK PLAY-ALONG

Alligator Bogaloo • The Chicken • Cissy Strut • Cold Duck Time • Comin' Home Baby • Mercy, Mercy, Mercy • Put It Where You Want It • Sidewinder • Tom Cat • Watermelon Man.
00196728 Book with Online Media..........$17.99

6. SONNY ROLLINS PLAY-ALONG

Airegin • Blue Seven • Doxy • Duke of Iron • Oleo • Pent up House • St. Thomas • Sonnymoon for Two • Strode Rode • Tenor Madness.
00218264 Book with Online Media........$17.99

7. THELONIOUS MONK PLAY-ALONG

Bemsha Swing • Blue Monk • Bright Mississippi • Green Chimneys • Monk's Dream • Reflections • Rhythm-a-ning • 'Round Midnight • Straight No Chaser • Ugly Beauty.
00232768 Book with Online Media........$17.99

8. BEBOP ERA PLAY-ALONG

Au Privave • Boneology • Bouncing with Bud • Dexterity • Groovin' High • Half Nelson • In Walked Bud • Lady Bird • Move • Witches Pit.
00196728 Book with Online Media..........$17.99

9. CHRISTMAS CLASSICS PLAY-ALONG

Blue Christmas • Christmas Time Is Here • Frosty the Snow Man • Have Yourself a Merry Little Christmas • I'll Be Home for Christmas • My Favorite Things • Santa Claus Is Comin' to Town • Silver Bells • White Christmas • Winter Wonderland.
00236808 Book with Online Media..........$17.99

10. CHRISTMAS SONGS PLAY-ALONG

Away in a Manger • The First Noel • Go, Tell It on the Mountain • Hark! the Herald Angels Sing • Jingle Bells • Joy to the World • O Come, All Ye Faithful • O Holy Night • Up on the Housetop • We Wish You a Merry Christmas.
00236809 Book with Online Media..........$17.99

11. JOHN COLTRANE PLAY-ALONG

Blue Train (Blue Trane) • Central Park West • Cousin Mary • Giant Steps • Impressions • Lazy Bird • Moment's Notice • My Favorite Things • Naima (Niema) • Syeeda's Song Flute.
00275624 Book with Online Media........$17.99

12. 1950S JAZZ PLAY-ALONG

Con Alma • Django • Doodlin' • In Your Own Sweet Way • Jeru • Jordu • Killer Joe • Lullaby of Birdland • Night Train • Waltz for Debby.
00275647 Book with Online Media........$17.99

13. 1960S JAZZ PLAY-ALONG

Ceora • Dat Dere • Dolphin Dance • Equinox • Jeannine • Recorda Me • Stolen Moments • Tom Thumb • Up Jumped Spring • Windows.
00275651 Book with Online Media........$17.99

14. 1970S JAZZ PLAY-ALONG

Birdland • Bolivia • Chameleon • 500 Miles High • Lucky Southern • Phase Dance • Red Baron • Red Clay • Spain • Sugar.
00275652 Book with Online Media........$17.99

15. CHRISTMAS TUNES PLAY-ALONG

The Christmas Song (Chestnuts Roasting on an Open Fire) • Do You Hear What I Hear • Feliz Navidad • Here Comes Santa Claus (Right down Santa Claus Lane) • A Holly Jolly Christmas • Let It Snow! Let It Snow! Let It Snow! • The Little Drummer Boy • The Most Wonderful Time of the Year • Rudolph the Red-Nosed Reindeer • Sleigh Ride.
00278073 Book with Online Media........$17.99

HAL•LEONARD®
www.halleonard.com

Prices, content and availability subject to change without notice.

0919
333

The Best-Selling Jazz Book of All Time Is Now Legal!

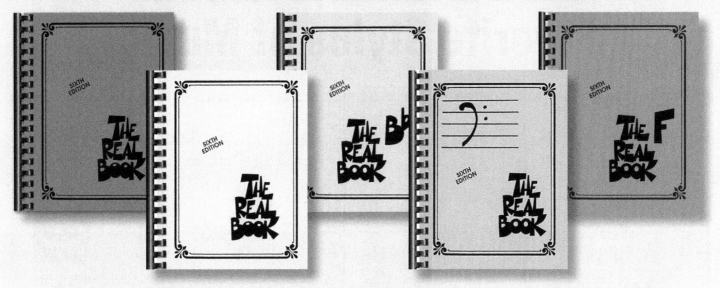

The Real Books are the most popular jazz books of all time. Since the 1970s, musicians have trusted these volumes to get them through every gig, night after night. The problem is that the books were illegally produced and distributed, without any regard to copyright law, or royalties paid to the composers who created these musical masterpieces.

Hal Leonard is very proud to present the first legitimate and legal editions of these books ever produced. You won't even notice the difference, other than all the notorious errors being fixed: the covers and typeface look the same, the song lists are nearly identical, and the price for our edition is even cheaper than the originals!

VOLUME 1
00240221	C Edition	$39.99
00240224	B♭ Edition	$39.99
00240225	E♭ Edition	$39.99
00240226	Bass Clef Edition	$39.99
00286389	F Edition	$39.99
00240292	C Edition 6 x 9	$35.00
00240339	B♭ Edition 6 x 9	$35.00
00147792	Bass Clef Edition 6 x 9	$35.00
00451087	C Edition on CD-ROM	$29.99
00200984	Online Backing Tracks: Selections	$45.00
00110604	Book/USB Flash Drive Backing Tracks Pack	$79.99
00110599	USB Flash Drive Only	$50.00

VOLUME 2
00240222	C Edition	$39.99
00240227	B♭ Edition	$39.99
00240228	E♭ Edition	$39.99
00240229	Bass Clef Edition	$39.99
00240293	C Edition 6 x 9	$35.00
00125900	B♭ Edition 6 x 9	$35.00
00451088	C Edition on CD-ROM	$30.99
00125900	The Real Book – Mini Edition	$35.00
00204126	Backing Tracks on USB Flash Drive	$50.00
00204131	C Edition – USB Flash Drive Pack	$79.99

VOLUME 3
00240233	C Edition	$39.99
00240284	B♭ Edition	$39.99
00240285	E♭ Edition	$39.99
00240286	Bass Clef Edition	$39.99
00240338	C Edition 6 x 9	$35.00
00451089	C Edition on CD-ROM	$29.99

VOLUME 4
00240296	C Edition	$39.99
00103348	B♭ Edition	$39.99
00103349	E♭ Edition	$39.99
00103350	Bass Clef Edition	$39.99

VOLUME 5
00240349	C Edition	$39.99
00175278	B♭ Edition	$39.99
00175279	E♭ Edition	$39.99

VOLUME 6
00240534	C Edition	$39.99
00223637	E♭ Edition	$39.99

Also available:
00151290	The Real Book – Enhanced Chords	$29.99
00282973	The Reharmonized Real Book	$39.99

HAL•LEONARD®

Complete song lists online at www.halleonard.com

Prices, content, and availability subject to change without notice.

REAL BOOKS
Now Available in Your Favorite Styles of Music!

The Real Books are the best-selling jazz books of all time. Since the 1970s, musicians have trusted these volumes to get them through every gig, night after night. The problem is that the books were illegally produced and distributed, without any regard to copyright law, or royalties paid to the composers who created these musical masterpieces. Hal Leonard is very proud to present the first legitimate and legal editions of these books ever produced – and now has also published brand new volumes with a blockbuster selection of songs in a variety of genres.

Also available:

00295069	The Real Bebop Book E♭ Edition	$34.99
00154230	The Real Bebop Book C Edition	$34.99
00295068	The Real Bebop Book B♭ Edition	$34.99
00240264	The Real Blues Book	$34.99
00310910	The Real Bluegrass Book	$35.00
00240223	The Real Broadway Book	$35.00
00125426	The Real Country Book	$39.99
00240355	The Real Dixieland Book C Edition	$32.50
00122335	The Real Dixieland Book B♭ Edition	$35.00
00294853	The Real Dixieland Book E♭ Edition	$35.00
00240268	The Real Jazz Solos Book	$30.00
00240348	The Real Latin Book C Edition	$37.50
00127107	The Real Latin Book B♭ Edition	$35.00
00118324	The Real Pop Book – Vol. 1	$35.00
00295066	The Real Pop Book Vol. 1 B♭ Edition	$35.00
00286451	The Real Pop Book - Vol. 2	$35.00
00240437	The Real R&B Book C Edition	$39.99
00276590	The Real R&B Book B♭ Edition	$39.99
00240313	The Real Rock Book	$35.00
00240323	The Real Rock Book – Vol. 2	$35.00
00240359	The Real Tab Book	$32.50
00240317	The Real Worship Book	$29.99

THE REAL CHRISTMAS BOOK

00240306	C Edition	$35.00
00240345	B♭ Edition	$32.50
00240346	E♭ Edition	$35.00
00240347	Bass Clef Edition	$35.00
00240431	A-G CD Backing Tracks	$24.99
00240432	H-M CD Backing Tracks	$24.99
00240433	N-Y CD Backing Tracks	$24.99

HAL•LEONARD®
Complete song lists online at
www.halleonard.com

Prices, content, and availability subject to change without notice.